You Are Magic

A Guided Journal to Unlock the Power of
Your Inner Unicorn, Llamacorn, and Narwhal

Tracey West

Illustrated by
Alice Potter

HARPER FESTIVAL
An Imprint of HarperCollins Publishers

HarperFestival is an imprint of HarperCollins Publishers.

You Are Magic
Copyright © 2020 by HarperCollins Publishers
All rights reserved. Manufactured in China.
No part of this book may be used or reproduced in any
manner whatsoever without written permission except in
the case of brief quotations embodied in critical articles
and reviews. For information address HarperCollins
Children's Books, a division of HarperCollins Publishers, 195
Broadway, New York, NY 10007.
www.harpercollinschildrens.com
Library of Congress Control Number: 2019955960
ISBN 978-0-06-297713-7

20 21 22 23 24   SCP   10 9 8 7 6 5 4 3 2 1
❖
First Edition

Unleash Your Inner Magic!

Are you on a creative quest to stand out like a unicorn?

Are you a born leader who's loyal to your herd like a llamacorn?

Or are you chill and go-with-the-flow like a narwhal?

The truth is, we all have a sprinkle of **UNICORN,** a sprinkle of **LLAMACORN,** and a sprinkle of **NARWHAL** inside us. Which one are you most like? Take the quiz on the next page to find out!

Then explore and develop all sides of your personality through **writing, doodling,** and **making** things.

Are you feeling **carefree** like a unicorn today, **take-charge** like a llamacorn, or **thoughtful** like a narwhal? You'll find prompts that suit all your different moods, along with ideas to **spark** your imagination, help you **relax,** and **inspire** you to get to know yourself and your friends better. **Because once you find balance among these energies, you can be your best self and live your best life—no matter what mood you're in!**

What Is Your Magical Type?

Circle the best answer to each question. At the end of the quiz, color in the chart to see which single-horned creature you're most like—or if you're a mix of all three!

1. What kind of weather do you dislike the most?
a. a bitter cold winter day

b. a damp, rainy day

c. a dry, hot day

2. On a team, you're the one who:
a. cheers everyone on

b. leads

c. is the most understanding when your teammates
make mistakes

3. Snow day! What do you do?
a. bundle up, go outside, and catch snowflakes on your tongue

b. go sledding or skiing

c. stay inside and drink cocoa

4. In a crowded room, you:
a. stand out from everyone else

b. get stressed out if it gets too packed

c. stick close to your friends

5. At the beach, you are most likely to:
a. join a game of beach volleyball

b. hang out under your umbrella

c. dive under the waves to keep cool

6. If someone asked you to sit still for five minutes, you would probably:
a. give up after thirty seconds

b. refuse to do it without a good reason

c. close your eyes and nap for ten minutes

7. You think that magic:
a. is real

b. comes from your imagination

c. is the feeling you get when you're with someone you love

8. For vacation, you'd love to:
a. explore the Egyptian pyramids

b. go mountain climbing

c. chill out by the ocean

9. Your friends say you are:
a. someone they can have fun with

b. someone they can count on

c. someone they can talk to about anything

10. Your favorite way to express your creativity is to:

a. paint or draw

b. make something, like a birdhouse or a cake

c. write a poem about your feelings

11. When something goes wrong, you usually:

a. start to freak out

b. make a plan to fix things

c. relax, because you know it will all work out

12. Which of these words describes you best?

a. mysterious   b. organized   c. kind

13. In class, you:

a. often daydream or fidget in your chair

b. pay attention and take good notes

c. only pay attention to subjects that really interest you

14. You're standing in line at the store and the person in front of you is taking forever. What do you do?

a. lose patience and get out of line

b. tap the customer on the shoulder and ask what the problem is

c. play a game on your phone until the line moves

15. You look for friends who:

a. will let you have your space when you need it

b. don't mind letting you be the one who makes decisions

c. you feel you have a deep connection to

When you've answered all the questions, color in a box for each question you answered, A, B, or C. Which creature are you most like? Which kind of energy could you use more of?

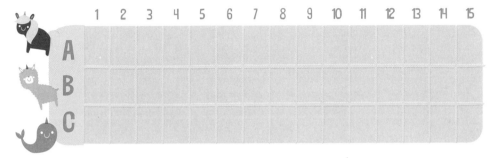

	1	2	3	4	5	6	7	8	9	10	11	12	13	14	15
A															
B															
C															

What the Types Mean

If you got mostly a's, you're a UNICORN

You are **creative** and **adventurous.** Your colorful personality and sense of **style** mean that you stand out in a crowd, whether you like it or not—just like a unicorn! You really want people to **believe** in you and your **ideas**. You enjoy **time alone,** but when you are around people, your **energy** and sense of **fun** is contagious.

You can teach others to: tap into their creativity, be independent, and think positively.

You might need help with: calming, grounding, focusing, and organizing.

If you got mostly b's, you're a LLAMACORN

You are **brave** and **passionate** about your beliefs. You are **determined** and ready to take on any challenge. Being a natural **leader** has given you **confidence.** You can **succeed** in almost any situation, just like a llamacorn, who is surefooted on any terrain. And you are **loyal** to your herd—your group of friends.

You can teach others to: organize, plan, and achieve their goals.

You might need help with: relaxing, letting your imagination run wild, learning how to slow down, and letting others lead.

If you got mostly c's, you're a NARWHAL

You are the most **centered** of this trio—and a bit of a **homebody. Gentle, loving,** and **calm,** you like to take things slow.
Narwhals dive deep into the ocean, and you are not afraid to dive deep into your **feelings.** Even though you need lots of **alone time,** your **friends and family** are very **important** to you.

You can teach others to: relax, be patient, be compassionate, and get in touch with their feelings.

You might need help with: getting motivated, picking up the pace, and taking risks.

6

How you use this journal is up to you. A **llamacorn** might start at the beginning and work through the book from start to finish. A **unicorn** might turn to a random page every time. And a **narwhal** might slowly browse through the journal, searching for the right page to fit their mood.

Each activity in the journal will have one or more of the **symbols** below. If you're feeling out of balance, try turning to a page that will help you tap into the **specific energy** you need.

Unicorn entries will give you a boost of creativity, fun, happiness, and energy.

Llamacorn prompts will inspire you to focus, take action, and get organized.

Narwhal pages will help you to chill, relax, and be kind to yourself and others.

These activities help you balance all three energies.

CREATURE FEATURES

Do you agree with your quiz results?

YES   NO   SORT OF

Which unicorn traits do you share?

_____
_____
_____

Which llamacorn traits do you share?

_____
_____
_____

Which narwhal traits do you share?

_____
_____
_____

My quiz results make me feel:

(Write, draw, or use color to show your feelings!)

UNIQUELY YOU

Unicorns, llamacorns, and narwhals all have one thing in common: they each have one horn. That horn represents all the things that make them stand out in a crowd. Draw or write about the things that make you uniquely you.

Close your eyes and imagine a horn growing out of your forehead. Is it big or small? Glittery or earthy? Straight or twisty? Decorate your one-of-a-kind horn!

Here and Now!

One day, you may look back on this journal and want to know more about the amazing person who wrote it. Answer these questions to help future you!

Today's date: _____

How old are you? _____

Who is your best friend? _____

What is your favorite color? _____

What is your favorite food? _____

What is your favorite song? _____

What is your favorite subject at school? _____

What is your favorite animal? _____

What is your favorite place? _____

What are your favorite hobbies? _____

_____

What is your favorite thing to do with friends?

_____

What is your favorite volunteer project?

_____

What is the biggest surprise you've had in this school year so far?

_____

_____

_____

What objects do you treasure the most?

_____

_____

_____

What do you look forward to the most every day?

_____

_____

_____

What do you like most about yourself right now?

_____

_____

_____

How do you hope to be even better in the future?

_____

_____

_____

Getting to Know You

Write or draw your answers to these questions.

When do you feel the happiest?

How do you like to help others?

What makes you stand out?

What scares you the most?

What are you curious about?

What makes you feel the most creative?

What makes you feel the calmest?

What makes you feel like taking charge?

your Name Is Magic!

Figuring out your magical name is a fun way to tap into your magic. Call on your magical name when you want to feel creative, brave, or strong.

Your Magical First Name

Circle the first letter of your name.

A: Allora
B: Bianca
C: Crystal
D: Diamond
E: Elvina
F: Flicker
G: Glimmer
H: Happy
I: Iris

J: Jewel
K: Kahoko
L: Lavender
M: Mystery
N: Nala
O: Opal
P: Pixie
Q: Questa
R: Rainbow

S: Sunshine
T: Treasure
U: Unity
V: Vega
W: Willow
X: Xyla
Y: Yulia
Z: Zabrina

Your Magical Middle Name

Circle the name of the amazing creature you're most like.

Unicorn   Llamacorn   Narwhal

Your Magical Last Name

Circle the month you were born.

January:
Light Maker

February:
Sweet Soul

March:
Tender Heart

April:
Springtime

May:
Hope Singer

June:
Green Hill

July:
Moon Star

August:
Quicksilver

September:
Blue Sky

October:
Silly Face

November:
Swift Stride

December:
Good Heart

My Magical Name Is:

Power Up!

What magical powers do you wish you had? How would you use them? Write or draw your answers below.

_____

_____

_____

_____

_____

Imaginary magical powers are awesome,
but you don't need magic to be magical.

CREATIVITY IS MAGIC!
CONFIDENCE IS MAGIC!
KINDNESS IS MAGIC!

What is your most magical quality?

_____

_____

_____

19

Once Upon A Time

Every legendary creature knows that books can take you to impossible, wonderful places.

**What are your favorite books?
What do you Love about them?**

Music Is Magic!

List five songs that cheer you up when you're sad.

1 _____
2 _____
3 _____
4 _____
5 _____

List five songs that pump you up and make you feel like dancing.

1 _____
2 _____
3 _____
4 _____
5 _____

List five songs that relax you.

1 _____
2 _____
3 _____
4 _____
5 _____

Listen to one of the songs you have listed.
While the song is playing, draw, doodle, or write
whatever pops into your mind.

Would You Rather. . . ?

Circle your best answer to each question.

climb a mountain **or** make a painting of a mountain?

get one wish granted **or** grant wishes to everyone you know?

stay up late **or** wake up early?

travel to the moon **or** to the bottom of the ocean?

be famous for inventing something **or** for doing something brave?

have one best friend **or** five close friends?

not speak for one day **or** not sleep for one day?

be famous on social media for being funny **or** for having good taste?

travel backward in time **or** travel forward to the future?

be a zombie in a scary movie **or** someone who fights the zombies?

have wings to fly **or** gills that let you breathe underwater?

have the power of invisibility **or** the power to read others' thoughts?

eat apple pie **or** pizza pie for breakfast for a whole month?

sneeze glitter **or** spit rainbows?

be the director of a film **or** the star?

be friends with a dragon **or** with a princess?

live in a log cabin in the woods **or** an apartment in a big city?

Make up your own would-you-rather questions here!

_____ or _____

_____ or _____

_____ or _____

_____ or _____

_____ or _____

Make It Happen!

Unicorns are great at coming up with ideas. If you could invent anything, what would it be and why? How would you make it? Write or draw your ideas.

YES I CAN!

Llamacorn types believe that they can do anything! When you need a boost of confidence, tap into your llamacorn energy by repeating one of these positive sayings out loud.

I will shine like a magical unicorn.

I will climb this mountain with the determination of a llamacorn.

I am as strong and graceful as a narwhal.

Now write your own power phrases.

Draw a picture of yourself as a magical unicorn, a powerful llamacorn, or a wise narwhal.

Keeping Your Cool

Sometimes narwhals can worry too much about what others think.

Write about a time something embarrassing happened to you. How did you react? How did you feel?

_____

_____

_____

_____

_____

_____

_____

_____

_____

Now imagine a unicorn friend is giving you a pep talk.
What would they say to remind you how AWESOME you are?

Gallop Into Adventure

Adventurous unicorns dream of traveling the world.

What is your fantasy vacation?

What are three adventures you could have with your friends this weekend?

33

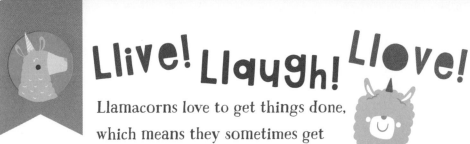

Llive! Llaugh! Llove!

Llamacorns love to get things done, which means they sometimes get upset when something stands in their way. They've even been known to spit rainbows when they're really mad!

Think about a time when you were **really** angry. What did you do to calm yourself down?

_____

_____

_____

_____

_____

_____

_____

_____

Now imagine your best narwhal friend was there to cheer you up! What would they say to make you feel sunny and sparkly again?

Rainbow Breathing

No matter what type you are, everyone feels low sometimes. If you need a boost of happiness, rainbow breathing can help.

Close your eyes and breathe in slowly through your nose. Breathe out and imagine a rainbow streaming out of your nose, sparkling in the light. **Keep breathing, and imagine the rainbow growing bigger until it stretches across a bright blue sky.**

Draw your rainbow here.

This or That? QUIZ

Narwhals **love to learn** more about themselves. For this quiz, circle the **first answer** that pops into your head. When you're done, **quiz a friend** and see how much you have in common!

Are you . . .

a dog **OR** a cat?

a bicycle **OR** a motorcycle?

a bowl of cereal **OR** a stack of pancakes?

an ice cream cone **OR** a birthday cake?

a violin **OR** a guitar?

a banana **OR** an orange?

a princess OR a pirate?

a waterfall OR a volcano?

a thunderstorm OR a gentle rain?

an elf OR a fairy?

a mouse OR an elephant?

a refrigerator OR an oven?

red OR blue?

a mountain OR a prairie?

a pillow OR a blanket?

fireworks OR a rainbow?

cotton candy OR popcorn?

Unicorn Doodling

When you doodle, you draw without thinking, letting your pencil take you wherever it wants to go. Unicorns love to doodle because it helps get creative energy flowing.

So grab your colored pencils, turn on some music, and doodle!

Sparkle in the Spotlight

Everybody is good at something—whether it's playing a sport or being a good listener. And confident llamacorns know their strengths. Write some things you're good at inside these stars.

What is something you want to get better at someday?

_____

_____

_____

43

MEMORIES ARE MAGIC!

Thoughtful narwhals remember all the good things that have happened to them.

What is your very first memory?
Write or draw it here.

_____

_____

_____

_____

What is your funniest memory?
Write or draw it here.

_____

_____

_____

_____

Top Three Things I Never Want to Forget:

1 _____

2 _____

3 _____

Dare to Dream

What would you do with a million dollars?

Buy a house and cover it with **glitter?**

Open an **animal rescue?** Learn to **fly?**

Tap into your **unicorn imagination** to come up with ideas and write or draw them here.

My Fantastic Future

Do you want to travel into **space** someday? Save lives in an **emergency** room? Host an **art** show? Llamacorns are great at **planning** for the future. What do you want your **future** to look like? **Write, draw, or scrapbook about it here.**

Dream Dive

What did you dream about last night? Plunge into your dream the way a narwhal dives deep into the ocean and write down everything you remember.

Write or draw a different ending to your dream.

What's the best dream you ever had?
Draw or write about it here.

What's the worst nightmare you ever had?
Draw a narwhal blasting it with a rainbow here.

Gallop with Glee

What things make you feel as happy as a winged unicorn soaring across a blue sky? Write them in these clouds.

Look at this page when you need a boost!

Brave Heart

Llamacorn types are good at things that take courage, like **meeting new people, being onstage,** or **trying new things.**

Write about a time you have been brave.

Now write about something you wish you had the
courage to face or do. Why do you want to do it?
What scares you most about it?

_____

_____

_____

_____

_____

_____

What would your best llamacorn friends say to help you feel brave?

_____

_____

_____

_____

LIONS AND TIGERS AND BEARS, OH MY!

Even though narwhal types need lots of alone time, they love to spend time playing with other sea creatures.

Imagine you could talk to animals. What would you ask them?

_____

_____

_____

_____

_____

_____

_____

_____

_____

_____

Narwhals love nature! Go outside and write a poem or draw a picture inspired by what you see.

THREE WISHES

You meet a unicorn with the power to grant wishes. You can make one wish for yourself, one wish for your best friend, and one wish for the world. What do you ask for?

My Wish for Me

My Wish for My Best Friend

_____
_____
_____
_____
_____
_____

My Wish for the World

_____
_____
_____
_____
_____
_____

LLOVE LLIKE A LLAMACORN

Llamacorns always look out for their herd.

What makes you a good friend?

_____

_____

_____

_____

_____

_____

_____

_____

Now think about your best friends.
What makes them magical?

_____

_____

_____

_____

_____

_____

Love Yourself

Narwhals know that before you can love anybody else, you have to love yourself!

Write one thing you love about yourself in each of these hearts.

Hearts for the Herd

Who makes up your herd? Write the names of your family members and friends in these hearts, and one thing you love most about each of them.

What are some things your friends and family members would say they love about you?

BRING ON THE GLITTER!

Painting, drawing, dancing, singing, writing—unicorns love to make the world shine with their creativity.

What is your favorite way to be creative?

_____

_____

_____

What's your favorite place to be creative?

_____

_____

What does your creative space sound like?
Do you blast music, or do you like things quiet?

_____

_____

_____

DESIGN YOUR OWN SUPER CREATIVE SPACE,
MEANT JUST FOR YOU AND YOUR IDEAS!
DRAW IT BELOW.

Go for It!

Reaching goals is like climbing a mountain. You keep going until you get to where you need to be—no matter how hard it gets.

What is one goal you'd like to reach?

What are some things you can do to reach that goal?

Draw yourself achieving your goal here.

Love Bubbles

Narwhal types are bubbling over with love and kindness—they've got plenty to go around!

Write messages of love to the world in these bubbles.

Now imagine them floating off the page and into the universe.

Sparkle Power!

When you feel positive, you can do anything you set your mind to!

Need a boost of happiness? Tap into your unicorn energy. Close your eyes and picture something that makes you happy. **Write or doodle it here.**

Are there any sounds or smells that make you smile? **Draw or write about them all here!**

Now list ten amazing things you could
do with your sparkling unicorn energy.

1 _____

2 _____

3 _____

4 _____

5 _____

6 _____

7 _____

8 _____

9 _____

10 _____

LLEAD LIKE A LLAMACORN

Llamacorns are natural leaders. Think about someone you know who is a great leader.

What makes them good at taking charge?
What do you admire most about them?

What qualities does this person have that you have, too?

Chill Out!

When you're feeling upset, angry, or just plain hyper, call on your narwhal energy.

WHAT ARE SOME THINGS YOU DO WHEN YOU NEED TO CALM DOWN?

WHAT KIND OF MUSIC MAKES YOU FEEL CHILL?

WHAT KINDS OF ACTIVITIES HELP YOU RELAX?

What Color Is Your Mood?

Does blue make you feel **peaceful** or **sad?** Does yellow make you feel **happy** or **anxious?**

Write down what color you associate with each mood.

Happy _____

Sad _____

Restless _____

Excited _____

Worried _____

Angry _____

Tired _____

Silly _____

Stressed _____

Peaceful _____

How are you feeling right now?
Fill in this rainbow with the colors of your mood.

Climb Every Mountain

Llamacorns may be **furry** and **cute**, but it takes a lot of **strength** to climb mountains like they do!

What makes you feel strong?
Draw or write about it here.

What are some things you can do to help your friends and family feel strong?

YOUR KIND HEART

When you perform an act of kindness, you are tapping into your narwhal energy.

Think about your friends and family.
What are some kind things you can do for them?

Now think about your community.
What's one thing you can do to make a difference in your neighborhood or at school?

It's just as important to be kind to yourself as it is to be kind to others. Write down some nice things you can do for yourself to say thank you for being you.

Uni-corny

What's the difference between a **carrot** and a **unicorn?** One is a bunny **feast.** The other is a funny **beast!**

What is the funniest thing that's ever happened to you? Draw or write about it here!

Who makes you laugh more than anyone else?

What else makes you giggle?

Make up a unicorn joke of your very own! Write it below.

Let Your Confidence Shine!

Confident llamacorns **believe** that they can do anything they set their **minds** to—and they are **okay** if their plans don't work out exactly how they **imagined** on the first try.

What is one thing you feel really confident about?

_____

_____

_____

_____

What is one thing you wish you felt more confident about?

_____

_____

_____

_____

_____

What do you do when you need
to feel more confident?

_____
_____
_____
_____
_____
_____

What's one thing you can do to help your friends to
feel more confident?

_____
_____
_____
_____
_____
_____

Ups and Downs

Just like narwhals float up and down on the ocean waves, life comes with highs and lows.

What has been the best day of your week so far?

Even narwhals have stormy days. Write everything that annoys you all over this page. Then scribble it all out until you feel better!

RAINBOW WINGS

You wake up one morning to find that rainbow wings have sprouted on your back. You can fly!

Fill in the comic panels to tell the story of what happens next.

WORD POWER

H◆pe! L◆ve! M◆gic! Power words like these can help you feel like you can do anything you set your mind to.

What words make you feel inspired, magical, and strong? Scribble your own power words all over this page.

JOY

Magic

Hope

LOVE

kindness

Write a poem, story, or song using one of your power words as the inspiration.

_____

_____

_____

_____

_____

_____

_____

_____

_____

_____

_____

_____

_____

_____

_____

_____

_____

_____

_____

_____

Gratitude Is Magic!

One way to float through life as relaxed and happy as a narwhal is to practice gratitude. Every day for a week, write down the things you are most thankful for.

MONDAY

TUESDAY

WEDNESDAY

THURSDAY

FRIDAY

SATURDAY

SUNDAY

Circle anything that comes up more than once.

Think about something really hard you have to do.

What are three things you can be grateful for even when times are tough? Look back at this list whenever you're having a bad day.

1. _____

2. _____

3. _____

Writing sprint

If your unicorn energy is **high** today, there might be a million **creative ideas** swirling around in your head. Set them free! Write down **anything** and **everything** that comes into your head in the next five minutes. **ANYTHING!**

Ready? Go!

Idea Clouds

Unicorns have so many ideas that they sometimes lose track of them—but llamacorns know the best way to remember things is to write them down.

Write your best ideas in these clouds, and they'll always be within reach

99

MOVEMENT IS MAGIC!

Moving your body can help you feel happier, more energized, and even relaxed.

What activity helps you tap into your happy unicorn energy?

_____

_____

_____

Do you like any sports? What activities help you tap into your competitive llamacorn side?

_____

_____

_____

What activity makes you feel centered like a narwhal?

_____

_____

Draw yourself moving your body
in your favorite way.

Power Posing

Try these yoga poses to connect with the magical energy you need right now. Before you begin, take off your shoes and put on some flexible clothing.

Charge up your unicorn energy with **Child's Pose**—and get ready to sprint through your day!

Boost your llamacorn energy—and your confidence—with **Mountain Pose!**

Relax into your narwhal self by lying with your back on the floor and your **Legs Up On The Wall!**

Fashion Is Magic!

Who needs a **magic spell** when you've got a closet and an **imagination?** Clothes can give you **confidence,** show off your **personality,** or reflect your **mood.** That's pretty magical!

What is your favorite item of clothing?

_____

_____

What do you wear when you want to feel comfortable?

_____

_____

What clothes make you feel ready to take on the world?

_____

_____

Design an outfit or accessory
inspired by a unicorn,
Llamacorn, or narwhal.

your space is magic!

What kind of environment makes you feel like your most magical self? **TAKE THIS QUIZ TO FIND OUT!**

1. What's your ideal magical home?
a. castle

b. cabin in the woods

c. gingerbread house

2. Choose a color palette:
a. gold and silver

b. green and blue

c. bright rainbow colors

3. Everything can use a little more . . .
a. glitter

b. flowers

c. sprinkles

4. Choose a word:
a. glamorous

b. cozy

c. cheerful

5. What's one thing your magical home has to have?
a. ballroom

b. library

c. pool with a twisty slide

If you answered mostly a's, then you'd be happiest in a fancy, glittery home. If you chose mostly b's, you find magic in nature. If you chose mostly c's, you want a colorful home with lots of fun things to do.

Now draw or describe your dream house.

Is it the one you chose in the quiz, or something different, like an undersea cave or a treehouse?

Lucky You!

Unicorns and rainbows are symbols of good luck.

Fill in the rainbow with things that make you feel lucky.

What's the luckiest thing that's ever happened to you?

_____

_____

_____

If you don't feel lucky, what is one thing you could do to change your luck?

_____

_____

_____

Do you have a good luck charm? Draw one here.

NO MORE DRAMA, LLAMA!

Sometimes unicorns can get caught up in **gossip** or **fights** with their friends. But llamacorns are usually pretty good at avoiding all kinds of drama.

How does drama make you feel?

_____

_____

_____

_____

_____

_____

_____

_____

Tap into your llamacorn energy and ask yourself: What are some ways you can avoid drama at school and at home?

_____

_____

_____

_____

Write about a time you
helped to end an argument
between friends. What did you say?

FUN WITH FRIENDS

Think about a day when you and your best friend did something you never want to forget. Write, draw, or scrapbook about it here.

What new memory would you like to create with your friend?

Friends Are Magic!

Unicorns, llamacorns, and narwhals might be different in some ways, but they all **love their friends.** Now that you know which **creature** you're most like, ask your **friends** and **family** to take the **quiz** at the beginning of the book. Then write their results below.

Name: _____

Creature: _____

What makes them sparkle: _____

Name: _____

Creature: _____

What makes them sparkle: _____

Name: _____

Creature: _____

What makes them sparkle: _____

Name: _____

Creature: _____

What makes them sparkle: _____

Name: _____

Creature: _____

What makes them sparkle: _____

Name: _____

Creature: _____

What makes them sparkle: _____

Name: _____

Creature: _____

What makes them sparkle: _____

FUN WITH FRIENDS!

Unicorns, llamacorns, and narwhals LOVE hanging out with their friends.

Draw or paste a picture of you
and your friends having the most ↓
fun ever here.

Are most of your friends just like you or really different from you?

_____

If you wanted to make friends with a llamacorn, what would you do?

_____

_____

_____

What's something nice you could do for a narwhal friend?

_____

_____

_____

If your unicorn bestie was feeling down, how would you cheer them up?

_____

_____

_____

Magic in the Air

A spritz of **magical room spray** can lift your mood, help you focus, or relax you, depending on which essential oils you use.

This mix is for room spraying only! It is **not** for drinking.

You'll need:

* **1 small spray bottle, around 4 to 6 ounces**

* **Purified water**

* **4 to 6 drops of essential oils (see scent ideas on the next page)**

Add the water and essential oils to the bottle. Shake it up to mix. Then spray around the room.

For a unicorn spray to uplift your mood: use vanilla, lavender, orange, or a mix of all three.

For a llamacorn spray to help you focus: use peppermint, lemon, basil, or a mix of all three.

For a narwhal spray to help you sleep: use chamomile, lavender, bergamot, or a mix of all three.

What are some of your favorite smells? How do they make you feel? What do they remind you of?

_____

_____

_____

_____

Parties Are Magic!

Now that you and your friends know all about each other, put your **unicorn, llamacorn,** and **narwhal** brains together to plan the best party ever!

What is the theme of your party?

Where will the party be?

How will you decorate?

What will you eat?

Invent a new game for your party:

Name:

How to play:

Draft a playlist for your party:

Draw the invitation here.

RAINBOW TREAT

What do you feed **unicorns, llamacorns,** and **narwhals** when they come over?

A rainbow treat!

Make these rainbow gelatin cups with your friends. They take some **patience,** so you may need some narwhal energy—or an **adult**—to help out!

YOU'LL NEED:

8 10-ounce clear plastic cups

6 boxes gelatin in different flavors and colors (orange, grape, lemon, lime, cherry, and blueberry are good choices)

6 cups water

6 cups ice cubes

Can of whipped cream

EQUIPMENT YOU'LL NEED:

Small baking sheet

Heat-proof bowl

Kettle to boil water

Measuring cup

Measuring spoon (tablespoon)

DIRECTIONS:

1. Pour one flavor of gelatin into the heat-proof bowl and add 1 cup of boiling water. This will be the bottom of your rainbow.

2. Stir until the gelatin powder is dissolved.

3. Add 1 cup of ice cubes and stir until the ice cubes are melted.

4. Set up the plastic cups on the baking sheet.

5. Add about 3 tablespoons of the colored gelatin to each of the plastic cups. Put the cups in the freezer until the gelatin sets. This should take 10 to 12 minutes.

6. While the first layer is freezing, choose your next color. Repeat steps 1 to 4. When the first layer is set, pour 3 tablespoons of the new color of gelatin on top of the first layer.

7. Repeat until all six layers are set. Keep the rainbow treats covered with plastic wrap in the fridge until you're ready to serve them topped with a whipped-cream cloud.

Simple Smoothies

Want to show your friends you care? Whip up a smoothie created to help balance the energies in their magical type!

SUNNY UNICORN SMOOTHIE

1 cup banana yogurt

½ cup coconut milk

1 cup pineapple juice (unsweetened)

½ sliced banana

1 chopped mango (no peel or seed)

½ teaspoon cinnamon

Add the ingredients to the blender in the above order. Blend until smooth.

COOLING LLAMACORN SMOOTHIE

1 cup milk or almond milk

½ cup vanilla yogurt

1 tablespoon honey

1½ cups frozen mixed berries (such as strawberries, blueberries, and raspberries)

Add the ingredients to the blender in the above order. Blend until smooth.

CLEANSING NARWHAL SMOOTHIE

1 cup frozen sliced peaches

1 cup frozen sliced mango

½ cup frozen or fresh strawberries

1 cup orange juice

1 cup water (as needed)

Add the fruit and orange juice to the blender. Blend, adding water as needed to get the consistency you want.

FREE WRITING

Now that you know all about your amazing self—and your magical friends—write, draw, or scrapbook whatever you like on the following pages.

127